How to Have Fun
with Letters

Stewart Cowley

For a free color catalog describing Gareth Stevens Publishing's list of high-quality books and multi-media programs, call 1-800-542-2595 (USA) or 1-800-461-9120 (Canada). Gareth Stevens Publishing's Fax: (414) 225-0377. See our catalog, too, on the World Wide Web: http://gsinc.com

Library of Congress Cataloging-in-Publication Data

Cowley, Stewart.
  How to have fun with letters / by Stewart Cowley.
    p. cm. -- (Art smart)
  Includes index.
  Summary: Presents a variety of projects with writing, including scrolls, collage writing, secret codes, and edible writing.
  ISBN 0-8368-1711-7 (lib. bdg.)
  1. Handicraft--Juvenile literature. 2. Penmanship--Juvenile literature. 3. Alphabet in art--Juvenile literature. Drawing--Technique--Juvenile literature. [1. Handicraft. 2. Alphabet in art. 3. Drawing--Technique.] I. Title. II. Series.
TT160.C696 1997
745.5--dc20
                            96-35301

First published in North America in 1997 by
Gareth Stevens Publishing, 1555 North RiverCenter Drive, Suite 201, Milwaukee, Wisconsin, 53212, USA.
Original © 1996 by Regency House Publishing Limited (Troddy Books imprint), The Grange, Grange Yard, London, England, SE1 3AG. Text and illustrations by Stewart Cowley. Additional end matter © 1997 by Gareth Stevens, Inc.

Printed in the United States of America

1 2 3 4 5 6 7 8 9 01 00 99 98 97

Gareth Stevens Publishing
MILWAUKEE

Writing for Fun

Wherever you are — at home, in the car, at school, walking down the street — you can see writing. Writing is on billboards, street signs, store fronts, walls, windows, trucks, newspapers, magazines, books, posters, boxes, cans, and bottles — almost everywhere, in every possible size, style, and color!

This book will give you plenty of ideas on how to make your writing more decorative and fun. You will learn how to write in code and send secret messages. You will be able to make writing projects, such as letters, invitations, cards, and notes, exciting to write and read.

The ideas in this book are just the beginning. Once you discover that there's more to writing than ordinary styles and straight lines, you'll be able to create your own original work. Writing will never be the same again!

A Few Hints

Practice your printing. First, draw three lines on a piece of paper in pencil. Then, print the alphabet slowly and smoothly, making your letters even and rounded. Tall letters like *t* and *l* and capital letters reach the top line. Shorter letters, like *a* and *e*, remain at or below the middle line.

To help you write in straight lines, turn the paper slightly. If you are left-handed, turn the paper so that the bottom points to the left. If you are right-handed, point the bottom of the paper to the right.

Before you start any writing project, practice with different pens, pencils, and paper. Select a certain firmness of the lead in your pencil for a light or dark look. Some ink pens are designed to make thin lines, and some make broad strokes. Choose the best color of ink for your project. Some types of paper absorb more ink than others. A trial run will give you the result you want.

Writing Instruments

There are various kinds of pencils, pens, and other writing instruments available. These include:

- Regular pencils in varying firmness of lead
- Mechanical pencils
- Colored pencils
- Crayons (sharpened to a point or used blunt)
- Ballpoint pens
- Felt-tip and fiber-tip pens
- Fountain pens (with cartridges of ink or with ink from a bottle)
  - Quill pens (for dipping directly into ink)
  - Calligraphy pens (with specially shaped nibs, or tips. The nibs come in different sizes for drawing thin and thick strokes. Left-handed versions are available. Calligraphy pens work well when drawing decorated letters.)

You can also use pens and pencils that produce white or gold, silver, and other metallic colors. These look best on black or other dark-colored paper.

4

Paper

Some of the types of paper you can use for the projects in this book include:

- Plain white paper
- Thin cardboard
- Construction paper
- Newspaper
- Magazine paper
- Wax paper

Ancient paper
To make a piece of modern paper look like an old parchment or treasure map:

1. Tear a thin strip off each edge of a sheet of plain white paper.
2. Place the sheet of paper in a large dish so that it lies flat.
3. Pour in enough cold tea to cover the paper.
4. Soak the paper fifteen minutes.
5. Carefully lift the paper out of the tea, and hang it to dry.

Note: If you crease the paper before soaking it, the tea will stain the creases. This will make it look as if it had been in someone's pocket for years!

1 Color an entire piece of cardboard with crayon.

2 Mix some black paint with a little liquid soap.

3 Paint over the crayon.

4 Hang the cardboard until the paint is completely dry.

5 Use the end of a paper clip to scratch a note or picture on the cardboard.

6 The paint scratches off, showing the crayon underneath.

— YOU WILL NEED —
- Thin cardboard
- Crayons • Black paint
- Liquid soap • Paintbrush
- Paper clip

Use different colors of crayon to cover the cardboard. Then as you scratch your message, different colors will show through.

Scratch in pictures to decorate your message.

Robert's Room KEEP OUT

Scratch board

1 For a jigsaw invitation, write your invitation on a piece of cardboard.

2 Cut the invitation into several large pieces in various shapes.

3 Put the pieces in an envelope and send. Your guest has to complete the jigsaw to learn details about the party!

1 For a book invitation, fold two pieces of paper and a piece of cardboard in half.

2 Place the paper inside the cardboard. Sew or staple along the inner fold.

3 Decorate the book with drawings. Write details of the party on the inside pages.

– YOU WILL NEED FOR BOOK –
- Thin cardboard
- 2 pieces of paper
- Strong needle and thread; or stapler and staples
- Pens and paints

Use colored cardboard for the cover of the book. Decorate the cover and inside with pictures of balloons, cakes, and other colorful items cut from old magazines.

– YOU WILL NEED FOR JIGSAW –
- Thin cardboard
- Pens and paints
- Envelope
- Scissors

Party invitations

1 Write a message on a piece of paper.

2 Cut a strip of cardboard to the same width as the piece of paper.

3 Fold the strip in half. Tuck the paper inside the strip and glue it down.

4 Make a hole in the center of the paper just above the cardboard strip.

5 Thread some ribbon through, as shown.

6 Roll the paper up, starting from the top. Tie with the ribbon.

– YOU WILL NEED –
- Paper • Pen
- Strip of cardboard
- Glue • Scissors • Ribbon

If you want to send your message through the mail, place it in a cardboard tube. The tube inside an empty roll of paper toweling would be perfect. Don't forget to seal the ends.

Scroll

INVITATION

You are invited to a Party on 24th March to celebrate the Birthday of Paul Smith.

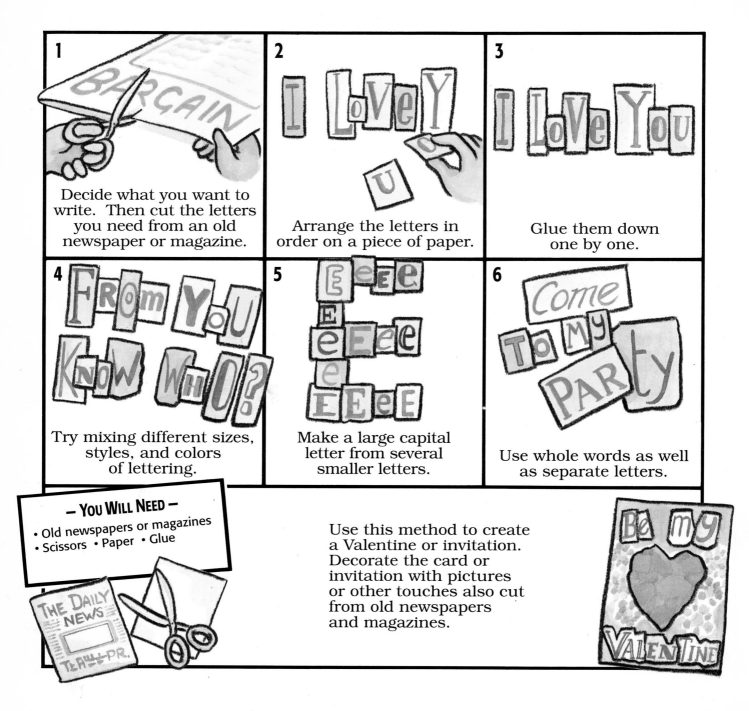

1
Decide what you want to write. Then cut the letters you need from an old newspaper or magazine.

2
Arrange the letters in order on a piece of paper.

3
Glue them down one by one.

4
Try mixing different sizes, styles, and colors of lettering.

5
Make a large capital letter from several smaller letters.

6
Use whole words as well as separate letters.

– You Will Need –
• Old newspapers or magazines
• Scissors • Paper • Glue

Use this method to create a Valentine or invitation. Decorate the card or invitation with pictures or other touches also cut from old newspapers and magazines.

Collage writing

1

Draw a large capital letter in any color.

2

Draw a design to fit the shape of the letter.

3

TREE

After you have finished your design, write the word to describe it.

1

R

Try another large capital letter in any color.

2

Decorate on and around it with curls and scrolls in different colors.

3

Rachel

Write the rest of the word.

– YOU WILL NEED –
- Pencil • Colored pencils
- Felt-tip pens • Paper
- Eraser

To keep your letters straight and neat, draw them in with a regular pencil first. Fill in with color later.

Decorated letters will make almost anything look grand. Try them on party invitations, letters, greeting cards, posters, and more!

Decorated letters

1

A B C D E
F G H
K L M

Write the alphabet on a sheet of paper.

2

A ... D E
F G H I J

Underneath each letter, write a number that becomes the key to your secret code.

3

A B C D E
1 2 3 4 5
F G H I J
6 7 8 9 10

For example, A=1, B=2, C=3, and so on. With this code, the word *big* is written as *297*.

4

A B C D E
B C D E F

Give each letter another letter. For example, A=B, B=C, C=D, and so on. With this code, the word *bed* is written as *CFE*.

5

A B C D E
Z Y X W V

Or make a code using the alphabet back to front, so that A=Z, B=Y, C=X, and so on. With this code, the word *bad* is written *YZW*.

6

A B C D E F G H I
1 2 3 4 5 6 7 8 9
J K L M N O P Q R
10 11 12 13 14 15 16 17 18
S T U V W X Y Z
19 20 21 22 23 24 25 26

8 9 / 4 / 22 9 4
8 15 23 / / 18 5

Use any code you want to create letters and words.

If you are writing a letter to someone in code, enclose the key, or explain what the first few words are.

EFBS NPOJLB
IBQQZ
CJSU IEBZ
MPWF
BOESFX

See if your friend can guess the code!

KEY
11·5·25
ENVELOPE
5·14·22·5·12·15·16·5/ 6·15·18
25·15·21·/18/19·53·18·5·
18·5·16··12·25

Secret codes

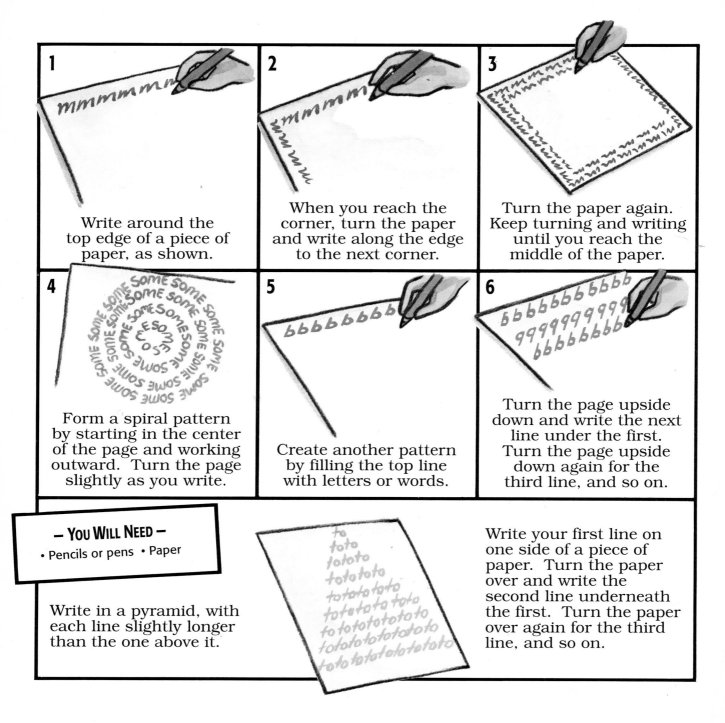

1 Write around the top edge of a piece of paper, as shown.

2 When you reach the corner, turn the paper and write along the edge to the next corner.

3 Turn the paper again. Keep turning and writing until you reach the middle of the paper.

4 Form a spiral pattern by starting in the center of the page and working outward. Turn the page slightly as you write.

5 Create another pattern by filling the top line with letters or words.

6 Turn the page upside down and write the next line under the first. Turn the page upside down again for the third line, and so on.

— YOU WILL NEED —
• Pencils or pens • Paper

Write in a pyramid, with each line slightly longer than the one above it.

Write your first line on one side of a piece of paper. Turn the paper over and write the second line underneath the first. Turn the paper over again for the third line, and so on.

Pattern writing

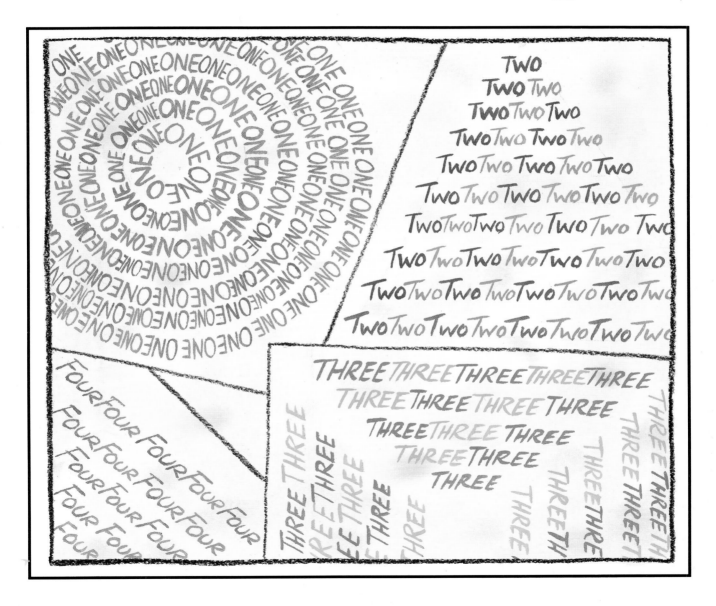

1 Practice making lines, curves, and thin and thick strokes with a calligraphy or quill pen.

2 Draw three pencil lines on a piece of paper. These lines will help you keep your letters even.

3 Find a style of writing you like from a book or magazine, or use the style shown here.

4 First, write the letters in pencil. Go over the pencil lines carefully in ink.

5 Wait until the ink is completely dry, then erase the pencil guidelines.

6 Decorate the letters with shading or coloring and by adding curls and scrolls.

— YOU WILL NEED —
- Calligraphy pen or quill pen
- Paper • Pencil • Ruler
- Eraser • Ink

You can make your own quill pen from a feather. Have an adult help you cut away and split the end, as shown. Keep dipping the quill in ink as you write. Careful — it can be messy!

20

Decorative writing

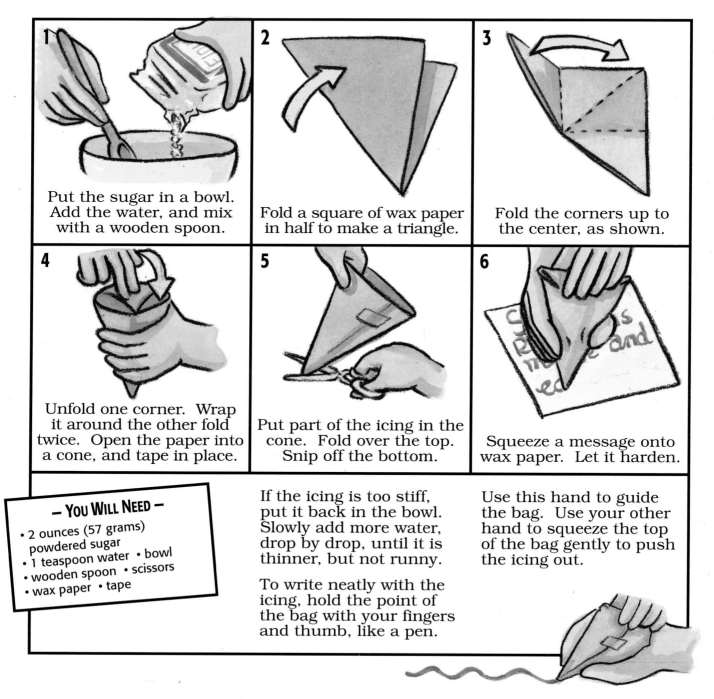

1 Put the sugar in a bowl. Add the water, and mix with a wooden spoon.

2 Fold a square of wax paper in half to make a triangle.

3 Fold the corners up to the center, as shown.

4 Unfold one corner. Wrap it around the other fold twice. Open the paper into a cone, and tape in place.

5 Put part of the icing in the cone. Fold over the top. Snip off the bottom.

6 Squeeze a message onto wax paper. Let it harden.

– YOU WILL NEED –
- 2 ounces (57 grams) powdered sugar
- 1 teaspoon water • bowl
- wooden spoon • scissors
- wax paper • tape

If the icing is too stiff, put it back in the bowl. Slowly add more water, drop by drop, until it is thinner, but not runny.

To write neatly with the icing, hold the point of the bag with your fingers and thumb, like a pen.

Use this hand to guide the bag. Use your other hand to squeeze the top of the bag gently to push the icing out.

Edible writing

More Books to Read

Codes. Nigel Nelson (Thomson Learning)
Draw, Model, and Paint (series). (Gareth Stevens)
Draw Write Now. Marie Hablitzel and Kim H. Stitzer (Barker Creek)
Drawing with Letters and Numbers. Syd Hoff (Scholastic)
Super Secret Code Book. Fran Pickering (Sterling)
Worldwide Crafts (series). (Gareth Stevens)

Videos

The Alphabet in Art. (Phoenix/BFA Films and Video)
Codes. (Altschul Group)
Letters. (Phoenix/BFA Films and Video)
Numbers and Letters. (Good Times Home Video)
Papercrafts One: Creative Correspondence. (Walk Away Entertainment)

Web Sites

http://www.go-interface.com/fridgeartz
http://finalfront.com/kids/art/art.htm

Index